Atkins Diet

Cookbook

The Complete Guide to Atkins Diet!

BY: Nancy Silverman

My Heartfelt Thanks and A Special Reward for Your Purchase!

https://nancy.gr8.com

My heartfelt thanks at purchasing my book and I hope you enjoy it! As a special bonus, you will now be eligible to receive books absolutely free on a weekly basis! Get started by entering your email address in the box above to subscribe. A notification will be emailed to you of my free promotions, no purchase necessary! With little effort, you will be eligible for free and discounted books daily. In addition to this amazing gift, a reminder will be sent 1-2 days before the offer expires to remind you not to miss out. Enter now to start enjoying this special offer!

Table of Contents

Chapter 1 - Snack Ideas

||||||||||||||||||||||||||||||||||||||||||||||||||||||||||||||||||||||||||

Zucchini Savory Muffins

Unlike other muffins, this muffin is completely low in sugar content. Made mainly from zucchini and cheese, this muffin will be a great option for you who want to reduce the sugar intake. Absolutely, this muffin is Atkins friendly because it is low in carbs. Enjoy this muffin as many as you want and get the beneficial content.

Portion Size: 4

Total Prep Time: 45 Minutes

Ingredient List:

- ½ cup grated zucchini

- ¼ cup grated cheddar cheese

- ¾ cup almond flour

- ½ tsp. Italian herbs

- ¼ tsp. black pepper

- 4 organic eggs

- ¼ cup butter, melted

||||||||||||||||||||||||||||||||||||||||||||||||||||||||||||||||||

Methods:

1. Crack the eggs then place in a bowl.

2. Add Italian seasoning and black pepper to the eggs then using a mixer beat until incorporated.

3. Next, add almond flour into the mixing bowl then using a wooden spatula mix until combined.

4. After that, pour melted butter over the mixture then mix well.

5. Add the grated zucchini and stirs until just combined.

6. Pour the batter into the prepared muffin cups then bake for 25 minutes or until the top of the muffins are lightly golden.

7. Remove the muffins from the oven then let them cool.

8. Serve and enjoy!

Each serving contains 236 Calories, 2.6 g Net Carbs, 21.3 g Fats, 10 g Protein

Crispy Baked Zucchini

This snack is so easy to make and I can guarantee you can successfully cook this one. You can also do the same with other kinds of vegetables, such as eggplants or even carrots.

Portion Size: 4

Total Prep Time: 30 Minutes

Ingredient List:

- 2 lbs. zucchini

- 2 organic egg whites

- ¾ cup grated coconut

- ½ tsp. pepper

||||||||||||||||||||||||||||||||||||||||||||||||||||||||||||||||

Methods:

1. Preheat an oven to 375 °F then lines a baking sheet with parchment paper.

2. Crack the eggs then place in a bowl. Beat until incorporated.

3. In another bowl, place the grated coconut and black pepper then mix well.

4. Peel and cut the zucchini into sticks. Discard the seeds.

5. Dip each stick in the beaten egg then roll it in the grated coconut.

6. Place the coated zucchini on the prepared baking sheet then repeat with the remaining zucchini.

7. Bake the coated zucchini for about 25 minutes until the zucchini is tender inside but crispy outside.

8. Transfer to a serving dish then enjoys warm.

Each serving contains 33 Calories, 4.5 g Net Carbs, 0.7 g Fats, 3.4 g Protein

Mixed Fruits with Cashew Sour Sauce

The sour and spicy sauce for this fruit salad is amazing. For sure, it gives you a different sensation. Also, the fruits of this salad are flexible. You can mix and match the fruits according to your desire. However, the fruits should be fresh. Also, you have to choose the fruit with the firm texture. This fruit salad is also good to be consumed with ice cubes.

Portion Size: 4

Total Prep Time: 10 Minutes

Ingredient List:

- ¼ cup sliced green apple

- ¼ cup sliced cucumber

- ¼ cup sliced mango

- ¼ cup roasted cashew

- 2 Tbsp. tamarind water

- 2 Tbsp. water

- ½ tsp. red chili flakes

||||||||||||||||||||||||||||||||||||||||||||||||||||||||||||||||

Methods:

1. Place the sliced apple, cucumber, and mango in a bowl. Set aside.

2. Place cashew and red chili flakes in a blender then pour tamarind and water into the blender. Blend until smooth and incorporated.

3. Pour the cashew mixture over the fruits then toss to combine.

4. Serve and enjoy!

Each serving contains 60 Calories, 5.5 g Net Carbs, 4 g Fats, 1.5 g Protein

Cheesy Eggplant Rolls

This dish is very simple and easy. However, the taste and the nutrient content of the food are obviously great. You can have this dish as a snack to fill your gastric between the main meals. For sure, this dish is high in protein. As a variation, you can also fill the eggplant roll with sautéed ground chicken.

Portion Size: 4

Total Prep Time: 30 Minutes

Ingredient List:

- 2 medium eggplants

- 1 organic egg

- ¾ lb. cheddar cheese

||||||||||||||||||||||||||||||||||||||||||||||||||||||||||||||||

Methods:

1. Preheat an oven to 350°F then lines a baking pan with aluminum foil. Set aside.

2. Peel the eggplant then cut lengthwise into thin slices. Set aside.

3. Cut the cheddar cheese into sticks then place in a bowl. Reserve a little amount of cheese—grate the cheese (about 2 Tbsp. of grated cheese).

4. Place a cheese stick on an eggplant sheet then roll the eggplant. Prick using a toothpick. Repeat with the remaining eggplants and cheese sticks.

5. After that, crack the egg then place in a bowl. Beat the egg until incorporated.

6. Dip each rolled eggplant then arranges in the prepared baking pan.

7. Sprinkle grated cheese on top then bake for 15 minutes.

8. Remove the rolls from the oven then transfer to a serving dish.

9. Enjoy!

Each serving contains 221 Calories, 7.4 g Net Carbs, 15.3 g Fats, 13.1 g Protein

Crispy Kale Chips

It can be denied that almost everyone loves chips. No wonder, chips are delicious and appetizing. Unlike other chips—that are usually high in calorie, these kale chips are very low in calorie. However, the nutrient content in this kale chips cannot be ignored. For sure, kale contains many great nutrients that are good for the body metabolism.

Portion Size: 4

Total Prep Time: 30 Minutes

Ingredient List:

- 4 cups chopped kale

- 1 ¾ Tbsp. olive oil

- ¾ tsp. pepper

||||||||||||||||||||||||||||||||||||||||||||||||||||||||||||||||||

Methods:

1. Preheat an oven to 350°F then lines a baking sheet with parchment paper.

2. Place the chopped kale in a bowl then splash olive oil over the kale. Toss to combine.

3. Arrange the kale on the prepared baking pan then sprinkles pepper over the kale.

4. Bake for about 10 minutes until the kale is crispy.

5. Remove the kale from the oven then let it cool.

6. Store in a jar then enjoys!

Each serving contains 86 Calories, 7.3 g Net Carbs, 6.1 g Fats, 2 g Protein

Coconut Strawberry Smoothie

Strawberry is a popular fruit that is easy to find in the nearest grocery stores. Both frozen and fresh strawberry is good to consume. Having a glass of smoothie strawberry for your snack time is really a great choice for strawberry is full of fiber and antioxidant. As a low-calorie ingredient, strawberry is completely healthy for you.

Portion Size: 4

Total Prep Time: 5 Minutes

Ingredient List:

- 2 cups fresh strawberry

- 1 cup unsweetened coconut milk

- ½ cup ice cubes

||||||||||||||||||||||||||||||||||||||||||||||||||||||||||||||||||||

Methods:

1. Place the fresh strawberries in a blender.

2. Add ice cubes to the blender then pour coconut milk over the fruits. Blend until smooth.

3. Divide the smoothie into 4 glasses then serve immediately.

4. Enjoy!

Each serving contains 33 Calories, 5.5 g Net Carbs, 1 g Fats, 0.7 g Protein

Warm Apple Cinnamon

This is another way to consume apples. If usually, you eat apples just the way it is, this time, we add cinnamon and butter over the apples. With a simple treatment, this apple can be a tempting snack that you can enjoy alone or with friends. This apple dish is also great to be consumed warm and cold.

Portion Size: 4

Total Prep Time: 30 Minutes

Ingredient List:

- 2 fresh apples

- ½ tsp. cinnamon

- 1-½ tsp. water

- 3 tsp. butter

|||||||||||||||||||||||||||||||||||||||||||||||||||||||||||||||||

Methods:

1. Peel the apples then cut into wedges or anything, as you desired.

2. Place the apples in a saucepan then add water, half of the cinnamon, and butter into it.

3. Bring to a simmer until the apples are tender.

4. Transfer to a serving dish then enjoys!

Each serving contains 51 Calories, 7.2 g Net Carbs, 2.9 g Fats, 0 g Protein

Cinnamon Ginger Cookies

Ginger and cinnamon is a perfect blend of taste that you will enjoy. With almond flour as the main ingredient, for sure, this cookie is not only delicious but also soft and tender. Having a bite of this cookie will never enough for your tongue. Enjoy this almond cookie with cinnamon and ginger in your movie time.

Portion Size: 4

Total Prep Time: 30 Minutes

Ingredient List:

- 1 cup almond flour

- 3 Tbsp. coconut flour

- 3 tsp. ginger

- 3 tsp. cinnamon

- 1 organic egg

- ¼ cup butter

- 2 Tbsp. coconut oil

||||||||||||||||||||||||||||||||||||||||||||||||||||||||||

Methods:

1. Place butter and egg in a mixing bowl then using a hand mixer mix until just combined.

2. Add ginger, cinnamon, and coconut oil to the mixture then mix well.

3. Slowly stir in almond flour and coconut flour to the bowl then using a wooden spatula mix them all until becoming dough.

4. Preheat an oven to 275°F then lines a baking sheet with parchment paper.

5. Take about a spoonful of dough then roll until becoming a ball. Press the ball to become a coin then place on the prepared baking sheet. Repeat with the remaining dough.

6. Bake the cookies for about 20 minutes until the top of the cookies are lightly golden.

7. Once it is done, remove from the oven and let it cool for a few minutes.

8. Store in a jar with a lid then enjoy in your movie time.

Each serving contains 390 Calories, 14.4 g Net Carbs, 35 g Fats, 9.2 g Protein

Baked Fish Sticks

Fish stick? Who can refuse its delicacy? From children to adults will surely enjoy this dish. No wonder, the combination between the tender fish fillet and crispy coating, for sure, gives a delicious taste and special texture that will make your tongue dances. This recipe will also fit for other fish and also chicken. Enjoy this fish stick with homemade tomato sauce!

Portion Size: 4

Total Prep Time: 30 Minutes

Ingredient List:

- ½ lb. salmon fillet

- ¾ cup almond flour

- ½ tsp. pepper

- 1-cup water

- 2 tsp. olive oil

||||||||||||||||||||||||||||||||||||||||||||||||||||||||||||||||

Methods:

1. Preheat an oven to 325°F then lines a baking sheet with aluminum foil.

2. Combine the almond flour with pepper then mix well.

3. Cut the salmon fillet into stick then roll each stick in the almond flour.

4. Take the coated stick out from the almond flour then dip in the water.

5. After that, return the stick to the almond flour and roll it. Make sure that all of the sides of the stick are completely coated with almond flour.

6. Repeat with the remaining salmon sticks then arrange them on the prepared baking sheet.

7. Bake for about 20 minutes or until the stick is lightly golden.

8. Take the fish sticks out from the oven then transfer to a serving dish.

9. Serve and enjoy warm.

Each serving contains 126 Calories, 1.3 g Net Carbs, 8.5 g Fats, 12.2 g Protein

Cheesy Spinach Mushroom

Mushroom is known as one of the great antioxidants. All kinds of mushrooms are loaded with great nutrients that are good for the human body metabolism. This dish uses spinach and cheese as the topping. However, you can substitute the topping with anything according to your desires. Beef, poultry, pork, or seafood can be a great choice for the topping.

Portion Size: 4

Total Prep Time: 30 Minutes

Ingredient List:

- 12 mushrooms

- 3 tsp. butter

- ¼ cup chopped onion

- ¾ cup chopped spinach

- ¼ cup grated mozzarella

||||||||||||||||||||||||||||||||||||||||||||||||||||||||||||

Methods:

1. Cut the stem of the mushrooms then sets aside.

2. Preheat a skillet over medium heat then place butter into it.

3. Once the butter is melted, stir chopped onion then sautés until lightly golden and aromatic.

4. Add chopped spinach to the skillet then stirs until wilted. Remove from heat then sets aside.

5. Preheat an oven to 375°F then lines a baking sheet with parchment paper.

6. Fill each mushroom cap with the cooked spinach then place on the prepared baking pan. Repeat with the remaining mushrooms.

7. Top each mushroom with grated mozzarella cheese then bakes for 25 minutes until the cheese is melted.

8. Once it is done, transfer to a serving dish then enjoys!

Each serving contains 46 Calories, 2.7 g Net Carbs, 3.4 g Fats, 2.5 g Protein

Chapter II - Breakfast Ideas

llllllllllllllllllllllllllllllllllllllllllllllllllllllllllllllll

Original Almond Porridge

For sure, it is the most practical breakfast that you will ever have. You only need to spend a very short period of time to generate this beneficial breakfast. Not only practical, this dish also serves a great nutrient that will help you to do all your activities in the busy morning. If you like, you can serve this almond porridge with fresh fruits or low carbs granola.

Portion Size: 4

Total Prep Time: 5 Minutes

Ingredient List:

- 1 ½ cup unsweetened almond milk

- ¾ cup ground almond

- ½ tsp. cinnamon

- 1-Tbsp. butter

Topping:

- 2 Tbsp. sliced roasted almond

|||||||||||||||||||||||||||||||||||||||||||||||||||||||||||

Methods:

1. Pour the almond milk into a microwave-safe bowl. Microwave it for 2 minutes.

2. Next, add the almond flour to the bowl and microwave again for a minute.

3. When it is done, remove from the microwave then quickly stir in butter and cinnamon. Mix well.

4. Serve and enjoy warm.

Each serving contains 144 Calories, 4.8 g Net Carbs, 13.1 g Fats, 4.2 g Protein

Spinach Scrambled Egg

This recipe is great to be consumed in the induced phase of Atkins Diet. With this menu, you don't need to include the carb at all. Simply eat this for breakfast and you will be actively okay to go through your busy day without carbs. Add more spinach if you want. You can substitute the spinach with other leafy green vegetables if you like. Adding some chopped or ground garlic will also be great.

Portion Size: 4

Total Prep Time: 5 Minutes

Ingredient List:

- 1 tsp. coconut oil

- 4 organic eggs

- 1-cup spinach

- 1 Tbsp. chopped onion ring

- ½ tsp. pepper

||||||||||||||||||||||||||||||||||||||||||||||||||||||||||||||||

Methods:

1. Crack the eggs and drop into a bowl. Using a fork beat until incorporated then sets aside.

2. Preheat a saucepan over medium heat then pour coconut oil into the saucepan.

3. Once it is hot, stir in chopped onion and sautés until wilted and aromatic.

4. Add spinach to the saucepan and cooks until wilted.

5. Pour beaten egg over the spinach then quickly stir the eggs until becoming scrambles.

6. Season with pepper then cooks until the egg is set but still soft.

7. Transfer to a serving dish then serves immediately.

Each serving contains 76 Calories, 1g Net Carbs, 5.5 g Fats, 5.8 g Protein

Bell Pepper Frittata

Although you may need extra time to prepare this dish, this is a very tasty breakfast menu. You can also substitute the fresh plain yogurt with the same amount of coconut milk. It will produce totally different taste but for sure it is also delicious.

Portion Size: 4

Total Prep Time: 1 hour 45 Minutes

Ingredient List:

- 3 organic eggs

- 2 tsp. minced garlic

- 3 Tbsp. chopped onion

- ¾ cup sliced red bell pepper

- ¾ cup yellow bell pepper

- 2 tsp. olive oil

- ½ cup sliced zucchini

- ¼ cup plain yogurt

- ¾ tsp. pepper

||||||||||||||||||||||||||||||||||||||||||||||||||||||||||||||||

Methods:

1. Crack the eggs then place in a bowl. Add yogurt to the eggs then beat until incorporated.

2. Preheat a pan over medium heat then pours olive oil into it.

3. Once it is hot, stir in chopped onion and minced garlic then sautés until wilted and aromatic.

4. Add bell pepper and zucchini into the pan then sautés until wilted.

5. Pour the egg mixture over the bell pepper and zucchini then spread evenly. Remove from heat then covers with aluminum foil.

6. Preheat an oven to 325°F then bakes the frittata for an hour.

7. After an hour takes the pan out from the oven then uncover it.

8. Return to the oven back then bakes for 30 minutes until the top of the frittata is lightly golden.

9. Remove from the oven then transfer to a serving dish.

10. Cut the frittata into wedges then serve. Enjoy!

Each serving contains 100 Calories, 6.4 g Net Carbs, 5.9 g Fats, 5.9 g Protein

Coconut Pancake

Coconut is a great healthy fat that you can consume. Coconut is not only natural, but also rich in vitamins and minerals. If you want more sensation and give a little touch of a tropical dish, you can shred some fresh coconut flesh to be chewed while enjoying the pancake.

Portion Size: 4

Total Prep Time: 5 Minutes

Ingredient List:

- ½ cup coconut flour

- 2 organic eggs

- ¼ cup coconut milk

- 1 tsp. coconut oil

|||||||||||||||||||||||||||||||||||||||||||||||||||||||||||||||

Methods:

1. Place the entire ingredients in a mixing bowl.

2. Using a whisker mix until incorporated.

3. Next, preheat a pan over medium heat then brush the pan with coconut oil.

4. Drop about 2 Tbsp. of the mixture into the pan and make a pancake.

5. Cook the pancake for about 2 minutes then flips it. Cook again for another 2 minutes or until both sides of the pancakes are lightly golden.

6. Repeat with the remaining mixture then arranges the pancakes on a serving dish.

7. Serve and enjoy warm.

Each serving contains 83 Calories, 2 g Net Carbs, 7.2 g Fats, 3.4 g Protein

Avocado Tuna Salads

Avocado contains an unsaturated fat that is good for the body. Combining smooth and creamy avocado with tuna and tomato is a great idea. Tomato, which is known as a great antioxidant surely add the benefits of this dish. Not to mention, tuna that is high in good nutrition. Besides good for breakfast, this dish is also enjoyable for lunch.

Portion Size: 4

Total Prep Time: 15 Minutes

Ingredient List:

- 2 ripe avocados

- 1 cup cooked chopped tuna

- ¼ cup diced tomato

- 1 Tbsp. chopped onion

- ½ tsp. pepper

- 1 tsp. olive oil

- 3 tsp. lemon juice

||||||||||||||||||||||||||||||||||||||||||||||||||||||||||||||||

Methods:

1. Preheat a skillet over medium heat then pour olive oil into it.

2. Once it is hot, stir in chopped onion then sautés until translucent and aromatic.

3. Add tuna and tomato to the skillet then sautés until wilted.

4. Season with pepper and lemon juice then stir well.

5. Remove the tuna from heat then let it cool for a few minutes.

6. Cut the avocados into halves then discard the seeds.

7. Scoop out the avocado flesh then combine it with the cooked tuna.

8. Fill the halved avocado with the tuna and avocado mixture then arranges on a serving dish.

9. Serve and enjoy right away.

Each serving contains 214 Calories, 8.4 g Net Carbs, 15.8 g Fats, 12.1 g Protein

Veggie Quiche

This quiche is full of protein and natural fiber. You can also find that this quiche is tasty and can satisfy your appetite at the same time. Feel free to substitute the kinds of vegetables you want. You can also cook it in a bigger baking pan if you don't have any muffin cup. This is a really simple recipe you can enjoy on the go.

Portion Size: 4

Total Prep Time: 30 Minutes

Ingredient List:

- ¾ Tbsp. olive oil

- 2 Tbsp. chopped onion

- 2 tsp. minced garlic

- 1 cup chopped kale

- ¼ cup diced bell pepper

- ¾ cup diced tomato

- 2 organic eggs

- 4 organic egg whites

- 1-½ Tbsp. milk

- ½ tsp. oregano

- ½ tsp. black pepper

||||||||||||||||||||||||||||||||||||||||||||||||||||||||||||

Methods:

1. Preheat an oven to 425°F then coat 8 muffin cups with cooking spray. Set aside.

2. Preheat a skillet over medium heat then pours olive oil into it.

3. Once it is hot, stir in chopped onion and minced garlic then sautés until aromatic and translucent.

4. Add kale, bell pepper, and tomato then stirs until wilted. Remove from heat.

5. Crack the eggs then place in a bowl.

6. Pour milk into the eggs then seasons with oregano and black pepper.

7. Add the sautéed vegetables to the egg mixture then mix well.

8. Divide the mixture into the 8 prepared muffin cups then bake for 20 minutes or until the eggs are set.

9. Remove the quiche from the oven then let them cool for a few minutes.

10. Take the quiche out from the cups then arrange on a serving dish.

11. Serve and enjoy immediately.

Each serving contains 95 Calories, 5.4 g Net Carbs, 5.1 g Fats, 7.6 g Protein

Broccoli Turkey Casserole

This casserole is rich in protein, vitamin, and fats. Therefore, this casserole is a good choice to support your Atkins diet. Feel free to substitute the vegetables and meat according to your desire. Also, put some herbs if you want another flavor. Another good thing from this casserole is that you can prepare it in advance and store it in your refrigerator. Once you want to consume it, you just simply need to microwave it and the casserole will be as delicious as before.

Portion Size: 4

Total Prep Time: 40 Minutes

Ingredient List:

- 1-cup broccoli florets

- 1 cup grated cheddar cheese

- 1 cup shredded cooked turkey

- 8 organic eggs

- 1 ½ tsp. black pepper

- ¼ cup chopped onion

- 3 tsp. butter

|||||||||||||||||||||||||||||||||||||||||||||||||||||||||||||

Methods:

1. Preheat an oven to 325°F then coats a casserole dish with cooking spray. Set aside.

2. Preheat a skillet over medium heat then place butter in it.

3. Once the butter is melted, stir in chopped onion and broccoli then sauté until the onion is aromatic and the broccoli is crispy.

4. Add cooked turkey to the skillet then mix well.

5. Transfer the mixture to the prepared casserole dish then spreads evenly. Set aside.

6. Crack the eggs then place in a bowl.

7. Season the eggs with pepper then beats until incorporated.

8. Pour the egg mixture over the broccoli and turkey then sprinkle grated cheese on top.

9. Bake the casserole for 30 minutes until the eggs are set.

10. Remove the casserole from the oven then serve warm.

Each serving contains 337 Calories, 3.7 g Net Carbs, 22.8 g Fats, 29.2 g Protein

Strawberry Rolls

It is the natural sweetness of strawberries that makes the recipe special. As an alternative, you can use other berries to smear the omelet. Great tip: don't mash the strawberries too softly, because strawberries chunks can add texture.

Portion Size: 4

Total Prep Time: 5 Minutes

Ingredient List:

- 3 organic eggs

- 1 tsp. olive oil

- 3 Tbsp. almond flour

- ½ cup strawberry

IIIIIIIIIIIIIIIIIIIIIIIIIIIIIIIIIIIIIIIIIIIIIIIIIIIIIIIIIIIIIII

Methods:

1. Crack the eggs and drop in a bowl.

2. Add almond flour to the egg then using a whisker mix the egg and almond flour until incorporated then sets aside.

3. Preheat a pan over medium heat then make 4 omelets on it.

4. Transfer the omelets to a flat surface then set aside.

5. Place the strawberries in a blender then blend until smooth.

6. Brush each omelet with strawberry then roll them.

7. Arrange on a serving dish then serve immediately.

Each serving contains 70 Calories, 1.9 g Net Carbs, 5.1 g Fats, 4.5 g Protein

Almond Soft Waffles with Cinnamon

It is true that this waffle contains lots of eggs. That is why; this waffle is so soft and moist. For sure, this waffle will be a great choice for your breakfast during the Atkins diet. Not only delicious but this waffle also high in protein and very low in carbs. Put extra topping on it to enhance the taste and appearance. Nuts, fresh fruits, and cheese will be a great option.

Portion Size: 4

Total Prep Time: 10 Minutes

Ingredient List:

- ¾ cup almond flour

- 3 organic eggs

- 2 Tbsp. olive oil

- ½ cup water

||||||||||||||||||||||||||||||||||||||||||||||||||||||||||||||||||

Methods:

1. Place the almond flour in the blender then pour water into the blender.

2. Crack the eggs then also place in the blender.

3. Next, add half of the cinnamon then blend them all.

4. Preheat a waffle maker then pour the mixture into it. Cook the waffle according to the machine directions.

5. Once it is done, arrange the waffles on a serving dish then enjoy!

Each serving contains 229 Calories, 5.2 g Net Carbs, 20.8 g Fats, 8.7 g Protein

Mushroom Omelet Black Pepper

Mushroom is known for its health benefit. It is rich in antioxidant that is proven to regenerate cells and fight cancers. Basically, you can use any mushrooms in this recipe. Combining several different mushrooms is great. This omelet is not only good to be served as breakfast, but you can also eat this as a snack.

Portion Size: 4

Total Prep Time: 5 Minutes

Ingredient List:

- 4 organic eggs

- ½ cup chopped mushroom

- ½ tsp. black pepper

- 2 Tbsp. chopped onion

- 4 tsp. chopped leek

- 1 tsp. olive oil

||||||||||||||||||||||||||||||||||||||||||||||||||||||||||||

Methods:

1. Crack the eggs and drop into a bowl.

2. Add chopped onion, mushroom, and ¼ tsp. black pepper then mix well.

3. Preheat a pan over medium heat then brush with olive oil.

4. Pour a quarter of the mixture then sprinkle chopped leek over the egg.

5. Dust black pepper on top then cooks until the omelet is set.

6. Transfer the omelet to a serving dish then repeat with the remaining mixture.

7. Serve and enjoy warm.

Each serving contains 78 Calories, 1.4 g Net Carbs, 5.6 g Fats, 5.9 g Protein

Chapter III - Lunch Ideas

||||||||||||||||||||||||||||||||||||||||||||||||||||||||||||||||||

Baked Chicken and Vegetable Salads

It is a very simple baked chicken ever. You don't need to add lots of spices to the dish for the chicken is already delicious. For a healthier option, you can use organic chicken. Have this chicken with vegetable salads, as you desired and recharge your energy for the rest of the day.

Portion Size: 4

Total Prep Time: 30 Minutes

Ingredient List:

- 1 ½ lbs. skinless chicken breast

- 1 ½ Tbsp. olive oil

- 1 tsp. black pepper

||||||||||||||||||||||||||||||||||||||||||||||||||||||||||||||

Methods:

1. Preheat an oven to 400°F then lines a baking pan with aluminum foil. Set aside.

2. Brush the chicken breast with olive oil then place in the prepared baking pan.

3. Sprinkle black pepper over the chicken then bakes for about 10 minutes.

4. After 10 minutes, flip the chicken then brush with the remaining olive oil.

5. Sprinkle black pepper as well as the other side then returns to the oven.

6. Bake for approximately 15 minutes or until the chicken is completely cooked and tender.

7. Transfer to a serving dish then enjoys with vegetable salads, as you desired.

Each serving contains 370 Calories, 0.3 g Net Carbs, 17.9 g Fats, 49.3 g Protein

Chicken Wings with Limes

Chicken wings have become everyone's favorite for it is tender and savory. This dish is an easy way to cook chicken wings without being fried. Not only for lunch, but these baked chicken wings are also perfect companion for your picnic. If you like a spicy taste, you can add more chili powder to the chicken wings.

Portion Size: 4

Total Prep Time: 50 Minutes

Ingredient List:

- 1-½ lbs. chicken wings

- 3 tsp. paprika

- 1 ½ tsp. chili powder

- ¾ tsp. oregano

- ½ tsp. pepper

- 3 tsp. olive oil

- 2 fresh limes

||||||||||||||||||||||||||||||||||||||||||||||||||||||||||||

Methods:

1. Preheat an oven to 375°F then lines a baking pan with aluminum foil.

2. Place paprika, chili powder, oregano, and pepper in a bowl then mix well.

3. Arrange the chicken wings in the prepared baking pan then brush with olive oil.

4. Season the chicken wings with the spice mixture. Shake if it is necessary.

5. Bake the chicken wings for approximately 45 minutes or until the chicken wings are completely cooked and tender.

6. Remove the baked chicken wings from the oven then transfer to a serving dish.

7. Cut one lime into halves then squeeze the juice over the chicken wings.

8. Cut another lime into wedges then sprinkle over the chicken wings as garnish.

9. Serve and enjoy warm.

Each serving contains 265 Calories, 5.3 g Net Carbs, 12.4 g Fats, 33.5 g Protein

Steamed Cabbage Rolls

This dish is one of the most practical but delicious lunches to have. It is not only practical but also healthy. Being very low in cholesterol and saturated fat, cabbage is a great choice for those who want to reduce the risk of having cardiovascular diseases and stroke. Moreover, cabbage is rich in iron, calcium, and potassium that is good for the body metabolism. You can prepare this dish in advance and store it in the freezer. When you want to eat it, you just have to steam it for about 10 minutes. Enjoy!

Portion Size: 4

Total Prep Time: 30 Minutes

Ingredient List:

- ½ lb. cabbage

- 1 lb. ground chicken

- 2 tsp. minced garlic

- 3 Tbsp. chopped onion

- ½ tsp. pepper

- 1 tsp. olive oil

- ½ cup water

||||||||||||||||||||||||||||||||||||||||||||||||||||||||||||||||||||||||||

Methods:

1. Preheat a steamer over medium heat then steam the cabbage leaves until wilted.

2. Remove the wilted cabbage leaves from the steamer then let them cool for a few minutes.

3. Meanwhile, preheat a skillet over medium heat then pour olive oil into it.

4. Once it is hot, stir in chopped onion and minced garlic then sautés until wilted and aromatic.

5. Add ground chicken to skillet then pour water into it. Bring to boil.

6. Once it is boiled, reduce the heat then cooks until the water is completely absorbed into the chicken.

7. Season with pepper then remove from heat. Set aside.

8. Take a sheet of steamed cabbage leaf then drop about 2 Tbsp. of the chicken filling.

9. Roll the cabbage tightly then arrange in the steamer. Repeat with the remaining cabbage leaves and chicken.

10. Steam the rolled cabbage for about 7 minutes then remove from the steamer.

11. Transfer to a serving dish the serves warm.

Each serving contains 248 Calories, 5.2 g Net Carbs, 9.7 g Fats, 33.9 g Protein

Delicious Beef in Green Pepper

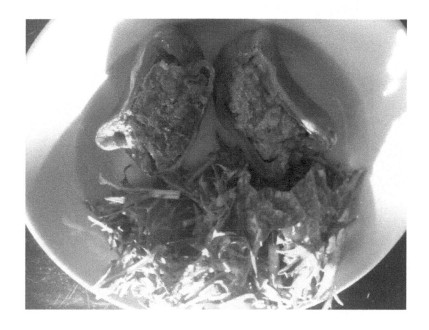

This is a delicious dish that will be ready for half an hour. The collaboration between beef and green pepper does not only give a special taste but also interesting appearance. If you don't have beef, chicken, pork, or fish can be a great substitution for this recipe. Besides that, you can also add vegetables, such as carrot or leek to enrich the nutrients.

Portion Size: 4

Total Prep Time: 30 Minutes

Ingredient List:

- 1-cup ground beef

- 1 tsp. minced garlic

- 1 tsp. olive oil

- ½ tsp. pepper

- 8 green peppers

- 3 organic eggs

||||||||||||||||||||||||||||||||||||||||||||||||||||||||||||||

Methods:

1. Preheat an oven to 350°F then lines a baking sheet with aluminum foil. Set aside.

2. Place ground beef in a bowl then season with minced garlic and pepper.

3. Add 2 eggs to the beef then mix until combined.

4. Cut the green peppers then discard the seeds.

5. Fill each green pepper with the beef mixture until full.

6. Crack the remaining egg then place in a bowl. Beat the egg until incorporated.

7. Dip each filled pepper in the beaten egg then arrange on the prepared baking sheet.

8. Baked for 20 minutes then take the baking sheet out from the oven.

9. Transfer the beefy peppers to a serving dish then enjoy!

Each serving contains 268 Calories, 11.7 g Net Carbs, 15.1 g Fats, 22.6 g Protein

Baked Turkey Balls

Perhaps you are not the fans of turkey. However, it will be changed since you try this balls recipe. This turkey balls for sure are juicy, tender, and perfect in color. For sure, once you taste them, it will become one of the staple foods in your family. Some people like to put oregano or other spices to enhance the taste. If you like traditional herbs, this is worth to try.

Portion Size: 4

Total Prep Time: 35 Minutes

Ingredient List:

- 1 lb. ground turkey

- 1 ½ tsp. olive oil

- ½ cup chopped onion

- 3 tsp. minced garlic

- 1 organic egg

- ½ tsp. pepper

||||||||||||||||||||||||||||||||||||||||||||||||||||||||||

Methods:

1. Preheat an oven to 375°F then lines a baking sheet with aluminum foil. Set aside.

2. Preheat a skillet over medium heat then pour olive oil into it.

3. Once it is hot, stir in chopped onion and minced garlic then sautés until translucent and aromatic. Remove from heat.

4. Transfer the sautéed onion and garlic to a bowl with ground turkey then add pepper and egg to the bowl. Mix well.

5. Shape the turkey mixture into medium balls forms then arrange in the prepared baking sheet.

6. Bake for 25 minutes or until the meatballs are completely cooked.

7. Transfer to a serving dish then enjoys warm.

Each serving contains 262 Calories, 2.3 g Net Carbs, 15.3 g Fats, 32.7 g Protein

Spicy Pork in Wrap

If you are often busy during the lunch hour, this dish is a good option. You can eat it while you are reading or doing something. Besides for lunch, this dish is also a perfect breakfast. It is a very practical dish that you can have on the go. If you like you can add paprika or mushroom to the filling.

Portion Size: 4

Total Prep Time: 30 Minutes

Ingredient List:

- 3 organic eggs

- 1 tsp. olive oil

- 3 Tbsp. coconut flour

- 2 Tbsp. coconut milk

- 1 cup diced cooked pork

- 1 tsp. minced garlic

- 2 Tbsp. chopped onion

- ½ tsp. black pepper

- ½ cup diced tomato

- 1 ½ Tbsp. red chili flakes

||||||||||||||||||||||||||||||||||||||||||||||||||||||||||||||

Methods:

1. Crack the eggs and drop into a bowl.

2. Add coconut flour and coconut milk to the eggs then using a whisker mix the egg and almond flour until incorporated then sets aside.

3. Preheat a pan over medium heat then make 4 omelets on it.

4. Transfer the omelets to a flat surface then set aside.

5. Preheat a skillet over medium heat then pour olive oil in it.

6. Once it is hot, stir in minced garlic and chopped onion then sautés until wilted and lightly golden.

7. Add red chili flakes together with the diced pork and tomato then season with black pepper.

8. Once it is done, remove from the heat then let it sit.

9. Divide the pork into 4 equal parts then place each part on an omelet.

10. Roll the omelet then place on a serving dish.

11. Repeat with the remaining omelets and filling then arrange them all in the serving dish or the lunch box.

12. Enjoy.

Each serving contains 195 Calories, 9.9 g Net Carbs, 9.4 g Fats, 17.6 g Protein

Beef Ball Soup

If you are a soup fanatic, this beef ball soup is really a great choice. The delicious beef balls in light but tasty gravy will surely make you addicted to. Add some red chili flakes or ginger to the soup to enhance the taste. This soup is also a great partner when you are having cold. It will warm your throat for sure. If you lack of beef, you can also use pork or chicken as the substitution. You can also add other vegetables that you like to the soup.

Portion Size: 4

Total Prep Time: 25 Minutes

Ingredient List:

- 1 lb. ground beef

- 1-quart water

- 2 cups low sodium beef broth

- 1 Tbsp. almond flour

- 3 tsp. minced garlic

- ½ tsp. pepper

- 1 cup chopped collard green

- 3 tsp. fried shallot

|||||||||||||||||||||||||||||||||||||||||||||||||||||||||||||||

Methods:

1. Pour water into a pot then bring to boil.

2. Meanwhile, place the ground beef and almond flour in a food processor. Pulse to combine.

3. Shape the mixture into small ball forms then drop into the boiling water. Wait until the meatballs are floating then remove from the boiling water.

4. Discard the water from the pot then pours beef broth into the pot.

5. Season the beef broth with minced garlic and pepper then bring to boil.

6. Once it is boiled, add chopped collard green and the meatballs to the pot then bring to a simmer.

7. Transfer the soup to a serving bowl then sprinkle fried shallot in top.

8. Serve and enjoy right away.

Each serving contains 255 Calories, 3.1 g Net Carbs, 9.3 g Fats, 37.8 g Protein

Fish Roll Tender

You don't need to be a chef to generate this delicious food. This fish roll is very flexible. You can eat it just the way it is, or fry it, or put it in a light soup. To enrich the nutrients content, you can also include vegetables or shrimps into the roll. This dish is best to be served with homemade tomato sauce

Portion Size: 4

Total Prep Time: 30 Minutes

Ingredient List:

- 1 lb. fish fillet

- 5 organic egg whites

- 3 tsp. minced garlic

- ½ tsp. pepper

||||||||||||||||||||||||||||||||||||||||||||||||||||||||

Methods:

1. Place the fish fillet in a food processor then add minced garlic and pepper. Pulse until the fish fillet is smooth and completely seasoned.

2. Transfer the smooth fish fillet to a bowl then add egg whites to the bowl. Mix well.

3. Prepare a sheet of aluminum foil then place on a flat surface.

4. Place the fish fillet mixture it then shape into a log.

5. Wrap the fish fillet with the aluminum foil then steam over medium heat for about 25 minutes.

6. Once it is done, remove the fish log from the steamer then let it cool.

7. Once the fish log is cool, unwrap it and cut into thick slices.

8. Arrange on a serving dish then enjoy warm!

Each serving contains 115 Calories, 1.2 g Net Carbs, 0.1 g Fats, 24.7 g Protein

Kale Salad Garlic with Egg

Kale is a super healthy vegetable that contains vitamin and mineral that is good for the body. Combine kale with garlic that has been known as cancer prevention generates a perfect combination of beneficial food. Enjoy this kale garlic with sunny sides up on top. For the best serving, I recommend ordering runny sunny sides up.

Portion Size: 4

Total Prep Time: 15 Minutes

Ingredient List:

- 4 cups chopped kale

- 2 Tbsp. minced garlic

- 2 tsp. olive oil

- 4 organic eggs

- ¼ tsp. black pepper

||||||||||||||||||||||||||||||||||||||||||||||||||||||||||||||

Methods:

1. Preheat a pan over medium heat then make 4 sunny sides up. Sprinkle black pepper over each egg then sets aside.

2. Preheat a skillet over medium heat then pour olive oil into it.

3. Once it is hot, stir in minced garlic then sautés until lightly golden and aromatic.

4. Add kale to the skillet then cooks until the kale is wilted and tender.

5. Transfer the kale to 4 serving dishes then add a sunny side up to each dish.

6. Serve and enjoy warm.

Each serving contains 123 Calories, 8.8 g Net Carbs, 6.7 g Fats, 7.8 g Protein

Baked Coconut and Carrot Fritter

Both carrot and coconut contain good nutrients for the body. Collaborate them in a menu does not only serve delicious taste but also a perfect health combination. You can put them in your lunch box and eat it during your official travel. However, you can also have it on your desk with homemade tomato sauce. Add some beef, chicken, or pork if you want a meaty taste.

Portion Size: 4

Total Prep Time: 40 Minutes

Ingredient List:

- 1-¼ cups grated carrot

- ¾ cups grated coconut

- 2 Tbsp. cilantro

- 3 tsp. coconut flour

- ½ tsp. ginger

- 3 tsp. coconut oil

- 1 tsp. paprika

|||||||||||||||||||||||||||||||||||||||||||||||||||||||||||||||||

Methods:

1. Preheat an oven to 350°F then lines a baking sheet with parchment paper.

2. Place the grated carrot and grated coconut in a bowl.

3. Add cilantro and coconut flour to the bowl then season with ginger and paprika. Mix until combined.

4. Shape the mixture into medium patties then arrange on the prepared baking sheet.

5. Brush the fritters with coconut oil then bake for 20 minutes.

6. Flip all of the fritters and brush the other sides with the remaining coconut oil. Bake for another 20 minutes.

7. Once it is done, remove the fritters from the oven then transfer to a serving dish.

8. Serve and enjoy warm.

Each serving contains 96 Calories, 11.5 g Net Carbs, 10 g Fats, 2.4 g Protein

Chapter IV - Dinner Ideas

||||||||||||||||||||||||||||||||||||||||||||||||||||||||||||||||||

Pork Chops

Why should you go to a fancy restaurant if you can cook delicious pork at your lovely kitchen? Pork chop is a common dish that becomes everyone's favorite. The protein content in pork chop is undeniable. To enhance the nutrient consumption, you can serve pork chops with vegetables salads.

Portion Size: 4

Total Prep Time: 30 Minutes

Ingredient List:

- 4 bone in pork chops

- 1 tsp. black pepper

- 2 tsp. olive oil

||||||||||||||||||||||||||||||||||||||||||||||||||||||||||||||||||

Methods:

1. Preheat an oven to 325°F then lines a baking pan with aluminum foil. Set aside.

2. Brush the pork chops with olive oil then sprinkle black pepper over the pork chops.

3. Place the seasoned pork chops in the prepared baking pan then bake the pork chops for about 30 minutes.

4. Once the pork chops are done and tender, take the baking pan out from the oven then transfer the pork chops to a serving dish.

5. Serve and enjoy right away.

Each serving contains 261 Calories, 1.3 g Net Carbs, 14.4 g Fats, 29.1 g Protein

Onion Sautéed Beef

This is an easy and quick dinner to cook during your busy weeknights. To save your time, you can boil the beef in advance until is it just tender then store it in your refrigerator. Once you want to cook this dish, you don't need to do the first and second steps. However, you have to make sure that you keep the half-cooked beef correctly. Put it in a container with tight lid and do not open it too much.

Portion Size: 4

Total Prep Time: 50 Minutes

Ingredient List:

- 1-½ lbs. beef tenderloin

- 1 tsp. olive oil

- ¼ cup chopped onion

- 1 tsp. black pepper

- 2 cups water

- 1-½ tsp. chopped celery

||||||||||||||||||||||||||||||||||||||||||||||||||||||||||||

Methods:

1. Place the beef tenderloin in a pot then pours water to cover. Bring to boil.

2. Once it is boiled, reduce the heat then cook until the beef is tender.

3. Take the beef out from the pot then cut into slices. Set aside.

4. Preheat a skillet over medium heat then pours olive oil into the skillet.

5. Once it is hot, stir in chopped onion then sautés until wilted and aromatic.

6. Add the sliced beef to the skillet then stir well.

7. Season with black pepper then transfer the sautéed beef to a serving dish.

8. Sprinkle chopped celery over the beef then serves immediately.

9. Enjoy!

Each serving contains 248 Calories, 1 g Net Carbs, 11.6 g Fats, 33 g Protein

Roasted Asparagus

Perhaps, asparagus is quite smelly. However, if you can pass it, you will find lots of reasons why you should fill your platter with asparagus. The asparagus is for sure packaged with good vitamins as well as minerals. Also, the asparagus is a great source of fiber that will help you to reduce your weight. Moreover, asparagus is very low in calories. Involving asparagus in your diet is a great option.

Portion Size: 4

Total Prep Time: 25 Minutes

Ingredient List:

- 1 bunch asparagus

- 2-½ Tbsp. olive oil

- 2 tsp. minced garlic

- ½ tsp. black pepper

- 3 tsp. lemon juice

||||||||||||||||||||||||||||||||||||||||||||||||||||||||||||||

Methods:

1. Trim the asparagus then sets aside.

2. Preheat an oven to 400°F then lines a baking sheet with parchment paper.

3. Drizzle olive oil over the asparagus then toss to combine.

4. Place the asparagus on the prepared baking sheet then sprinkle minced garlic and black pepper on top.

5. Bake the asparagus for about 18 minutes or until the asparagus is tender.

6. Once it is done, take the baking sheet out from the oven then splash lemon juice over the asparagus.

7. Transfer to a serving dish then enjoy warm.

Each serving contains 96 Calories, 3.8 g Net Carbs, 7.2 g Fats, 1.9 g Protein

Spicy Kale with Sesame Seeds

Kale is a super food that is famous with its nutritional content. That is why; involving kale in your diet is not only correct but also beneficial. The vitamin, calcium, iron, and phytochemical contained in kale for sure will help your body metabolism process runs better. One tip in cooking this dish: do not overcook the kale.

Portion Size: 4

Total Prep Time: 10 Minutes

Ingredient List:

- 2 ½ cups chopped kale

- 3 tsp. minced garlic

- 2 Tbsp. chopped onion

- 1 Tbsp. red chili flakes

- 1 tsp. olive oil

- 1 Tbsp. sesame seeds

IIIIIIIIIIIIIIIIIIIIIIIIIIIIIIIIIIIIIIIIIIIIIIIIIIIIIIIIIIIIIIIII

Methods:

1. Place minced garlic, chopped onion, red chili flakes, and olive oil in skillet.

2. Preheat the skillet over medium heat then sautés those four ingredients until aromatic.

3. Add chopped kale to the skillet then cooks until the kale is tender.

4. Transfer the cooked kale to a serving dish then sprinkle sesame seeds on top.

5. Serve and enjoy!

Each serving contains 54 Calories, 6.1 g Net Carbs, 2.9 g Fats, 1.8 g Protein

Beef and Broccoli in Tomato Stew

Beef contains both protein and fats. For sure, this dish is a great choice for supporting the Atkins diet. Moreover, the tomato and broccoli are also rich in antioxidant that will help you to improve your health and prevent diseases at the same time. One tip for the broccoli: soak the broccoli in salt water for a few minutes to ensure that all caterpillars that are often in the broccoli's head are completely gone. After that, don't forget to wash and rinse the broccoli.

Portion Size: 4

Total Prep Time: 25 Minutes

Ingredient List:

- ½ lb. beef tenderloin

- 2 cups broccoli florets

- 2 cups water

- 1-cup tomato puree

- 3 Tbsp. chopped onion

- ½ tsp. pepper

- 1 tsp. olive oil

|||||||||||||||||||||||||||||||||||||||||||||||||||||||||||||||||||

Methods:

1. Cut the beef tenderloin into thin slices then sets aside.

2. Preheat a skillet over medium heat then pours olive oil into it.

3. Stir in chopped onion into the skillet then sautés until translucent and aromatic.

4. Next, add the sliced beef to the skillet then stir until the beef is no longer pink.

5. Pour water into the skillet then cook until the water is completely absorbed into the beef and the beef is tender.

6. Season with pepper then pours tomato puree over the beef. Bring to boil.

7. Once it is boiled, reduce the heat and stir in broccoli florets.

8. Cook for approximately a minute until the broccoli has just wilted.

9. Transfer to a serving dish then enjoy immediately.

Each serving contains 140 Calories, 7.8 g Net Carbs, 5.3 g Fats, 15 g Protein

Grilled Chicken with Green Pesto

Are you looking for an easy grilled chicken recipe? So, this is the answer. This grilled chicken is very easy to cook. Even, the beginner in cooking world is able to cook this dish well. The green pesto in this recipe also enhances the taste of the grilled chicken. You can make the green pesto in a large portion then store it in the refrigerator. Once you want to consume, you just have to thaw it while grilling the chicken.

Portion Size: 4

Total Prep Time: 50 Minutes

Ingredient List:

- 1-½ lbs. boneless chicken

- 1 tsp. minced garlic

- ½ tsp. pepper

- 1 tsp. olive oil

- ½ cup chopped parsley

- 2 ½ Tbsp. chopped basil

- 1 Tbsp. lemon juice

- 2 Tbsp. sesame oil

|||||||||||||||||||||||||||||||||||||||||||||||||||||||||||

Methods:

1. Cut the chicken into ¾ –inch thick slices then rub it with minced garlic and pepper.

2. Let the chicken sit for about 20 minutes then brush with olive oil.

3. Meanwhile, place chopped parsley, basil, lemon juice, and sesame oil in a food processor then pulse to combine.

4. Transfer to a container with a lid then store in the refrigerator.

5. Preheat a grill over medium heat and once it is hot, grill the chicken until completely cooked and lightly golden.

6. Place the grilled chicken on a serving dish then top with the green pesto.

7. Serve and enjoy.

Each serving contains 291 Calories, 1 g Net Carbs, 16.2 g Fats, 33.2 g Protein

Simple Shrimps Black Pepper Garlic

Shrimp is almost everyone's favorite. It is not only delicious but also easy to cook. The secret of this recipe is the freshness of the shrimps. Find the freshest shrimps in the nearest market and cook it as soon as possible. Also, do not overcook the shrimps. The shrimp will be moist, juicy, and crunchy if you just cook it a few minutes.

Portion Size: 4

Total Prep Time: 5 Minutes

Ingredient List:

- 1 lb. fresh shrimps

- 2 tsp. minced garlic

- ½ tsp. black pepper

- 1 tsp. olive oil

||||||||||||||||||||||||||||||||||||||||||||||||||||||||||||

Methods:

1. Peel the shrimps then set aside.

2. Preheat a skillet over medium heat then pours olive oil into it.

3. Once it is hot, stir in minced garlic then sautés until aromatic and lightly golden.

4. Add the peeled shrimps to the skillet then seasons with black pepper.

5. Sauté until the shrimps turn to pink then transfer to a serving dish.

6. Serve and enjoy warm.

Each serving contains 148 Calories, 2.4 g Net Carbs, 3.1 g Fats, 26 g Protein

Seafood Garlic in Blanket

It is nothing more special than a bowl of seafood on your dining table. Seafood is not only delicious but also beneficial. For sure, the omega 3 and other protein contained is seafood will help lower the risk of having cancer. You can mix all seafood in this recipe. However, if you don't like a kind of seafood, you can simply make it with just one or two favorite ingredients. Also, you can combine this sautéed seafood with vegetables, as you desired.

Portion Size: 4

Total Prep Time: 30 Minutes

Ingredient List:

- 2 organic eggs

- 1 tsp. olive oil

- 3 Tbsp. coconut flour

- 3 Tbsp. coconut milk

- 1-cup fresh shrimps

- ½ cup crab meat

- ¼ cup chopped squid

- 2 tsp. minced garlic

- 1 tsp. canola oil

- ½ tsp. pepper

||||||||||||||||||||||||||||||||||||||||||||||||||||||||||||||||

Methods:

1. Crack the eggs and drop into a bowl.

2. Add coconut flour and coconut milk to the eggs then using a whisker mix the egg and almond flour until incorporated then sets aside.

3. Preheat a pan over medium heat then make 4 thin omelets on it.

4. Transfer the omelets to a flat surface then set aside.

5. Preheat a skillet over medium heat then pour olive oil in it.

6. Once it is hot, stir in minced garlic then sautés until wilted and aromatic.

7. Add fresh shrimps, crabmeat, and chopped squid to the skillet.

8. Season with pepper then cooks until done.

9. Divide the sautéed seafood into 4 serving plates then top each plate with an omelet.

10. Serve and enjoy immediately.

Each serving contains 194 Calories, 8.7 g Net Carbs, 8.9 g Fats, 19.8 g Protein

Oxtail Soup

It is a hearty soup that is perfect and comforting anytime in any season. Made with special herbs, this soup offers an extra delicacy that will make your tongue dance. The secret of this soup is the tender of the oxtail. So, make sure to cook the oxtail until you don't need extra effort to bite it. If you like, you can also add carrot and celery to the soup. The carrot will give extra health benefit while the celery will serve extra tempting aroma of the soup.

Portion Size: 4

Total Prep Time: 2 Hours 15 Minutes

Ingredient List:

- 2 lbs. chopped oxtail

- 2 quarts water

- ¼ cup chopped onion

- 2 cloves

- 1 tsp. pepper

- ½ cup chopped leek

||||||||||||||||||||||||||||||||||||||||||||||||||||||||||

Methods:

1. Place the chopped oxtail in a pot then pour water into it. Bring to boil.

2. Once it is boiled, reduce the heat and cooks until the oxtail is tender.

3. When the oxtail is tender enough, season the soup with pepper, cloves, and onion. Bring to a simmer.

4. Add chopped leek just before serving then enjoy warm.

Each serving contains 571 Calories, 2.7 g Net Carbs, 30.1 g Fats, 70.3 g Protein

Baked Salmon with Parsley

It is no doubt that salmon is one of super fish with lots of nutrients content. Not only omega 3, salmon also supplies zinc, iron, niacin, and vitamin that are good for your body metabolism. Eating salmon once or twice a week is an easy way to improve your health.

Portion Size: 4

Total Prep Time: 30 Minutes

Ingredient List:

- 1 lb. salmon fillet

- 1 cup chopped parsley

- ¾ tsp. oregano

- 3 Tbsp. chopped onion

- 2 tsp. olive oil

- 3 tsp. minced garlic

- 4 Tbsp. lemon juice

Methods:

1. Preheat an oven to 375°F then lines a baking pan with aluminum foil. Set aside.

2. Splash the lemon juice over the salmon then let it sit for about 5 minutes.

3. Meanwhile, combine parsley with oregano, chopped onion, olive oil, and minced garlic then mix until combined.

4. Rub the salmon with the spice mixture then arrange on the prepared baking pan.

5. Bake the salmon for about 20 minutes or until the salmon is tender and no longer pink.

6. Once it is done, take the baking pan out from the oven then transfers the baked salmon to a serving dish.

7. Serve and enjoy warm.

Each serving contains 186 Calories, 2.8 g Net Carbs, 9.6 g Fats, 22.8 g Protein

About the Author

Nancy Silverman is an accomplished chef from Essex, Vermont. Armed with her degree in Nutrition and Food Sciences from the University of Vermont, Nancy has excelled at creating e-books that contain healthy and delicious meals that anyone can make and everyone can enjoy. She improved her cooking skills at the New England Culinary Institute in Montpelier Vermont and she has been working at perfecting her culinary style since graduation. She claims that her life's work is always a work in progress and she only hopes to be an inspiration to aspiring chefs everywhere.

Her greatest joy is cooking in her modern kitchen with her family and creating inspiring and delicious meals. She often says that she has perfected her signature dishes based on her family's critique of each and every one.

Nancy has her own catering company and has also been fortunate enough to be head chef at some of Vermont's most exclusive restaurants. When a friend suggested she share some of her outstanding signature dishes, she decided to add cookbook author to her repertoire of personal achievements. Being a technological savvy woman, she felt the e-book realm would be a better fit and soon she had her first cookbook available online. As of today, Nancy has sold over 1,000 e-books and has shared her culinary experiences and brilliant recipes with people from all over the world! She plans on expanding into self-help books and dietary cookbooks, so stayed tuned!

Author's Afterthoughts

Thank you for making the decision to invest in one of my cookbooks! I cherish all my readers and hope you find joy in preparing these meals as I have.

There are so many books available and I am truly grateful that you decided to buy this one and follow it from beginning to end.

I love hearing from my readers on what they thought of this book and any value they received from reading it. As a personal favor, I would appreciate any feedback you can give in the form of a review on Amazon and please be honest! This kind of support will help others make an informed choice on and will help me tremendously in producing the best quality books possible.

My most heartfelt thanks,

Nancy Silverman

If you're interested in more of my books, be sure to follow my author page on Amazon (can be found on the link Bellow) or scan the QR-Code.

https://www.amazon.com/author/nancy-silverman

CPSIA information can be obtained
at www.ICGtesting.com
Printed in the USA
LVHW032359040220
645831LV00001B/56